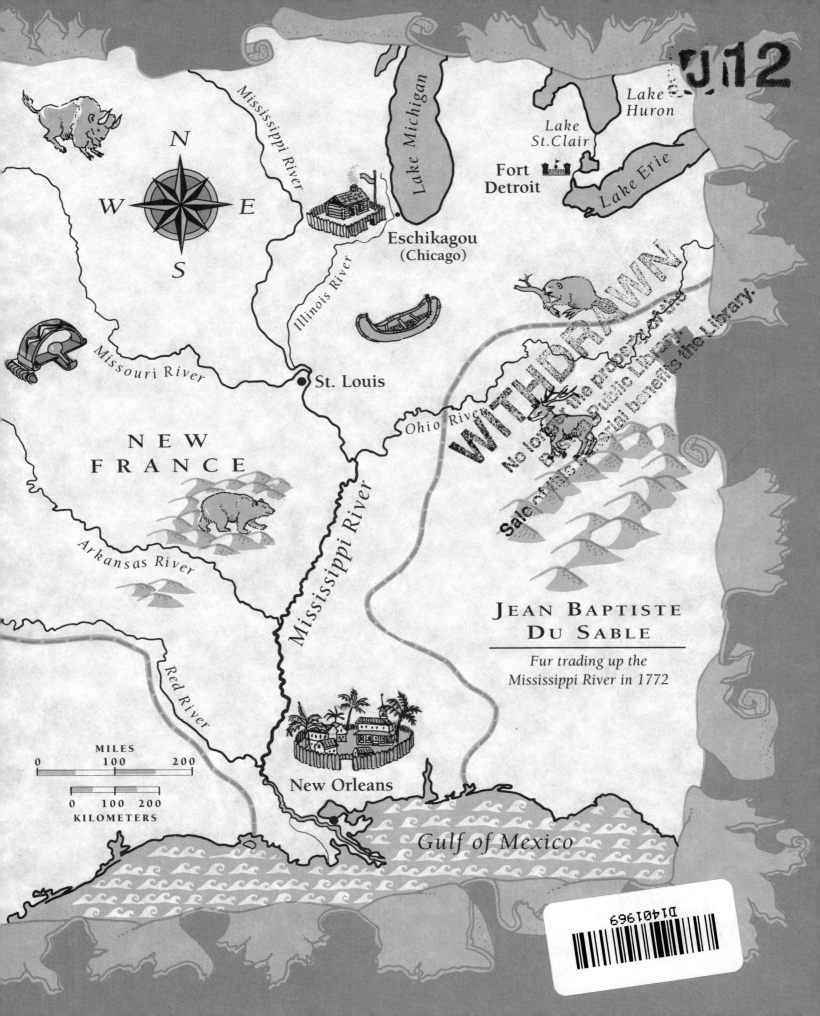

Mississippi River

N
W   E
S

Lake Michigan

Lake Huron

Lake St.Clair

Lake Erie

Fort Detroit

Eschikagou
(Chicago)

Illinois River

Missouri River

St. Louis

Ohio River

NEW FRANCE

Arkansas River

Mississippi River

Red River

JEAN BAPTISTE DU SABLE

Fur trading up the Mississippi River in 1772

New Orleans

Gulf of Mexico

MILES
0   100   200

0   100   200
KILOMETERS

THE STORY OF
JEAN BAPTISTE DU SABLE

BY ROBERT H. MILLER
ILLUSTRATED BY RICHARD LEONARD

Silver Press

This book is dedicated to my younger brother, Mancin Boyd, never stop dreaming   RHM

To my mother, Celia Martinez, and my daughter, Faviola A. Leonard   RL

To Ms. Toni Trent Parker, for suggesting this western series for young children. Thank you. Robert H. Miller.

Text copyright © 1995 Robert H. Miller
Illustrations copyright © 1995 Richard Leonard
Map copyright © 1995 Claudia Carlson
All rights reserved, including the right of reproduction in whole or in part in any form.
Published by Silver Press, Paramount Publishing, 250 James Street, Morristown, New Jersey 07960
Printed in the United States of America.
10 9 8 7 6 5 4 3 2 1

Library of Congress Cataloging-in-Publication Data
Miller, Robert H. (Robert Henry), 1944–
The story of Jean Baptiste Du Sable / by Robert H. Miller ; illustrated by Richard Leonard.
p.   cm.
ISBN 0-382-24392-7 (LSB)   ISBN 0-382-24402-8 (JHC)
ISBN 0-382-24397-3 (SC)
1. Pointe de Sable, Jean Baptiste, 1745?–1818—Juvenile literature.
2. Chicago (Ill.)—History—To 1875—Juvenile literature.   3. Pioneers—Illinois—Chicago—Biography—Juvenile literature.   4. Afro-American pioneers—Illinois—Chicago—Biography—Juvenile literature.   [1. Pointe de Sable, Jean Baptiste. 1745?–1818.   2. Pioneers.   3. Afro-Americans—Biography.]   I. Leonard, Richard, ill.   II. Title.
F548.4.P66M55   1995   977.3'11'02092—dc20   [B]   94-28634
CIP   AC

Author's Note

   Back in the 1700s there was a region in North America
known as New France. French explorers had claimed the land
and had named it to honor their homeland. At its southern tip
was the port city of New Orleans, on the Gulf of Mexico. From
there, French soldiers, traders, and explorers could journey
north to Canada. Many hoped to strike it rich by making their
way up the Mississippi River and selling the furs and other
goods they found there.

   Jean Baptiste Du Sable became a successful fur trader on
Lake Michigan. And he became the first to settle the place
we call *Chicago*.

Jean Baptiste Pointe Du Sable was born in St. Marc, Haiti, around 1745. His father, Pointe Du Sable, was a sailor. His mother, Suzanne, was a freed slave.

Once, when Jean Baptiste's father and most of the other men were at sea, the village was raided by a band of Spanish pirates.

"Run, run!" the villagers shouted. "The Spanish are killing everyone in sight!"

Jean Baptiste had been standing along the cliffs. He was waiting for some sign of his father's ship, which was due to return any day.

When he turned and saw the smoke of burning houses, Jean raced back home. Bursting inside, he found his mother lying still on the floor. Her neck had been broken by a Spanish pirate.

In confusion and despair, Jean Baptiste tried to think what he should do.

Racing back to the cliffs, young Jean saw the Spanish galleons docked near a hidden cove. They were waiting for his father's ship to come into the harbor so they could steal the goods on board, and kill the crew.

Jean could see the ship's sails on the horizon. He stripped off his shirt and took a deep breath. Then he leaped from the high cliffs into the ocean.

The ship's captain, El Negre, scanned the waters from his command post. "Man overboard! Man overboard!" he shouted.

A rope shot out from the bow. Jean Baptiste struggled to grasp it.

"Hang on, young fella!" shouted the crew as they pulled Jean on board.

"Jean! Jean, is that you?" asked his father, pushing his way through the crowd.

"Papa, the Spaniards are burning St. Marc," Jean gasped. "Their ships are waiting for you!"

El Negre heard what Jean said. Quickly, he gave the order, "Sail, ho!" The crew hurried into action, turning the ship around and out of harm's way.

Pointe asked cautiously, "Your mother, is she…?"

Jean told his father the sad news. Pointe Du Sable turned his head away and wept.

That was the last time Jean Baptiste Du Sable would ever see his homeland. By 1764, he had settled outside Paris, France. After he graduated from St. Cloud's boarding school, Jean was not sure what he wanted to do with his life. He had heard stories of a French colony in North America, called New France. The stories excited Jean's imagination.

Jean convinced a friend, Jacques Clemorgan to join him in seeking his fortune. They bought a small schooner, named it the *Suzanne*, and set sail for North America.

The trip across the ocean was rough. But when they reached the port city of New Orleans, the friends knew their journey had been worthwhile. Jean saw many small boats loaded down with trading goods. He saw fishing shacks and shops lined up along the wharf.

The city of New Orleans was surrounded by a wooden wall. Inside it, Jean glimpsed a tropical vista of palm trees and white buildings. It looked much like the island home he had left so long ago.

Jacques had taken ill on the journey, but Jean was full of energy. And he wanted to work.

One day, Jean heard that a trading company was hiring trappers and traders. They were going to send them up the Mississippi River to a northwest outpost called St. Louis.

Jean found the hiring place and walked up to the foreman. "I am a seaman," he said. "I can be very useful to your company."

The boss looked Jean over from head to toe. "Sorry, we don't have any more openings. Next!" the boss shouted.

Du Sable turned around and saw he was the only black man in line. Gathering up his pride, he walked out of the office. If *they* were going up the Mississippi to trap and trade, why couldn't *he*? Du Sable thought. All he needed was someone who knew the country.

Jean found his guide right away. He was a Choctaw Indian who knew the land around the Mississippi like the back of his hand. Together, the two men prepared for their journey.

First, they chopped down cottonwood trees and built a boat. Next, they rounded up guns, ammunition, and supplies. At last, they were ready to go.

As Jean and the Choctaw headed up the great river, the land around them changed like the colors of a rainbow. The men soon reached St. Louis, but decided to try their luck farther north. With fewer trappers and traders, there was more to be earned.

After traveling for days, the Choctaw motioned for Jean to pole their boat to shore. The men built a fire.

"We are in the land of the great chief Pontiac," the Choctaw told Jean. "He is a peaceful man. But the British will not listen to talk of peace. They only care for war, gold, and fur."

"Will there be a war with the British?" Jean asked.

"Before I came to New Orleans, Pontiac asked who would stand by him if he fought the British. Many Indian nations said they would stand with Pontiac," the Choctaw said proudly.

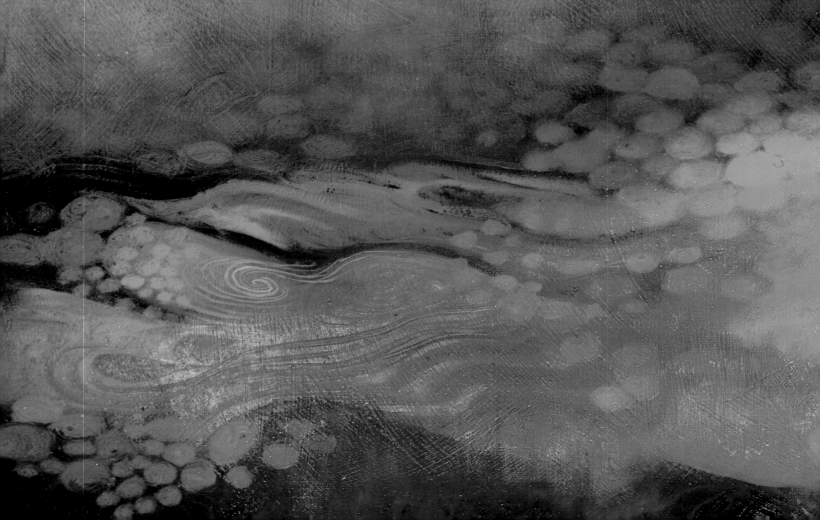

At that moment both men heard something rustling in the bushes. Jean reached for his gun, but he was too late. A strong hand gripped his arm. The Choctaw, too, struggled as three Indians held him down. Both men's hands were tied, and they were placed in a canoe. As Jean looked behind him, he saw two more canoes filled with Indians.

The men traveled a short distance, then pulled in to shore. The Indians led both men to a village. There was a cabin greater than anything Jean had ever seen.

Inside the cabin, several Indians stood before a platform. At its center was a tall, graceful Indian. Jean knew he was someone important.

The Choctaw turned to Jean and whispered, "Pontiac." Both men bowed.

Pontiac motioned for Jean to stand before him. He looked into his eyes. "How are you called?" Pontiac asked.

"I am Jean Baptiste Du Sable. I am a Frenchman. I come in peace."

"Listen, then, Jean Baptiste Du Sable. My people want only peace, but others bring war and killing. This land belongs to none of us. It is the land of the Great Spirit. We must protect it, not destroy it for gold and furs."

Jean agreed. "I, too, have been at the mercy of greedy adventurers. Long ago, they burned my village and killed my mother. We must try to live in peace."

Pontiac smiled. He had heard many men speak of peace. He had also heard many lies. But he knew this young Frenchman was speaking the truth.

The meeting marked the beginning of a friendship between young Jean and the great chief Pontiac. For the next two years, Jean was seldom away from Pontiac's side. He sharpened his hunting skills. He learned how to trap and ride wild horses. The Indians taught him how to track animals, from big buffaloes to small otters. By the time he left the village, Jean had become a true woodsman. He was ready to make his fortune in the fur business.

Jean decided it was time to find a piece of land to call his own. He had heard about some land around Old Fort Peoria that was for sale.

In the spring of 1772, with deed in hand, Jean walked
among the flowers and long grasses that covered his property.
Along the banks of Lake Michigan, he discovered an old,
broken-down log cabin. "With a little bit of work, this place
could be all right," Jean thought.

Jean set up camp on his new property. He soon noticed that many travelers passed by. Some were going up to Canada. Others were returning to the Mississippi Valley. It didn't take Jean long to figure out that a trading post on his property would do a booming business.

By 1779, business was doing so well that Jean built a large family house, a bake house, a dairy, a smokehouse, a stable, a workshop, and a horse-powered mill.

Jean got married that same year. His wife was a Potawatomi Indian named Kittihawa. Jean convinced her whole village to move onto his land. The trading post, his home, and the farm became the first buildings ever in this new place called *Eschikagou*.

Jean Baptiste Du Sable led a prosperous life in the fur-trading business. When he died, he left behind a daughter named Suzanne and a granddaughter named Eulalie. And he left the little town he founded. Eschikagou, or *Chicago*, had already begun to grow. And it hasn't stopped growing to this day.